JUST ONE MORE
TIME

JUST ONE MORE TIME

Jeffery Hayton

authorHOUSE®

AuthorHouse™
1663 Liberty Drive
Bloomington, IN 47403
www.authorhouse.com
Phone: 1-800-839-8640

First published by AuthorHouse   12/21/2011

ISBN: 978-1-4678-7923-1 (sc)
ISBN: 978-1-4678-7924-8 (ebk)

Printed in the United States of America

CONTENTS

PART ONE

Just One More Time As We Grow   1

PART TWO

Just one more time: before it's too late   33

PART THREE

Just one more time . . . It's too LATE?   75

PART ONE

Just One More Time As We Grow

A journey through growing up as a collection of experiences as a baby, a child, and teenager!

Just one more time spluttered the baby at mother's breast.
It really is the best!
Just one more time said the child to her older brother,
I want your toy not another!
Just one more time, said the bullying boys at school,
Or I'll tell teacher that YOU broke the rule.
Just one more time, said the lads discovering lust,
Oh go on we must!

Happy baby

With that beautiful scarlet hair,
And eyes coloured sapphire,
A dainty nose and a mouth,
With four teeth, north and south,
And a smile to steal your heart away
That's our pretty happy baby, today!

My first playgroup

I go to playgroup, and I think its kind-a cool,
My mum says, it's good preparation for school.
It's where I meet and learn to play with others,
But infections are there too: worrying for mothers!
My Grandma says some exposure can develop immunity
To any germs that are present in the community.
Sometimes I have a sore, or my tummy is in knots,
Sometimes I have had red marks that look like angry
spots!
But mainly I'm really healthy, there playing with new
friends,
Learning to get on with others, on which the future
depends.

My new baby walker

I have a brand new baby walker,
With a handle and 4 red wheels,
It has buttons which when I press,
Make a noise like music in a mess!
When I stop to listen and look around,
Sometimes I topple over and fall to the ground!

I have another baby walker,
A walking talking kind,
That talks to me using baby noises,
Pity, I would prefer grown up voices!
But I hold on tight to the stubby fingers,
Just for a moment it lingers
As it pulls me along,
It walks and talks, and sings a song.

Yes you must have guessed,
Granddad is my "best-est"
Baby walker!

Baby's new shoes

Pink is the colour of my new shoes,
Fitted with Velcro fasteners, I can use,
So I can put them on whenever I choose,
Happily, I walk everywhere in my new shoes!

Now I can walk round and about
Trying my brand new pink shoes out!
Looking like I own the town, there is no doubt,
Proudly, I walk everywhere in my new shoes!

Around the house I go treading on carpet and floor,
I do not trip over my feet as I have done before.
I climb the stairs head held high, I'm scared no more.
Confidently, I walk everywhere in my new shoes!

I can walk outside now that I'm steady,
I put on my new shoes whenever I'm ready.
It makes me feel smart, if a little light headed.
Boastfully I walk everywhere in my new shoes!

I ventured outside but the rain came down,
I thought I was so clever, I splashed around.
My new shoes got covered in mud from the ground,
Now carefully I look where I put new shoes!

Samuel Snail

Samuel Snail is a most colourful creature,
Who a looks at you as he comes to meet you,
With eyes on stalks, an unusual feature!
But he moves so very slow.

Samuel Snail does not put his laundry in a sack.
When it rains he has no need to ever wear a mac,
Because, he has his house strapped to his back.
That's why he moves so very slow.

Samuel Snail's has buttons so he can sing a song,
Pressing them in sequence else the tune goes wrong!
Other buttons can make the note short or long,
But still he moves so very slow.

Samuel Snail moves by sliding over the ground,
Slowly, quietly never ever making a sound!
I have looked and no feet or toes have I found!
Perhaps that's why he moves so very slow.

I like to copy Granddad

I like to copy Granddad,
He smiles with eyes wide open,
He shakes his head, and nods it too
It's fun to copy Granddad.

I like to copy Granddad
We play hide your face behind a chair-
Boo! Such a scare!
It's fun to copy Granddad

I like to copy Granddad
He likes toast and yoghurt, with more,
Crumbs and dairy liquid on the floor!
It's fun to copy Granddad

I like to copy Granddad
He spills his drink, drools and sneezes,
I even copy when he wheezes.
It's fun to copy Granddad

I like to copy Granddad
He goes to sleep mouth wide open,
A fly goes in, he chokes and coughs,
It's no more fun to copy Granddad.

My new wellies [1]

Do you remember I had my nice new shoes for walking out there!
Well guess what, my dad bought me a pair of nice Wellie [1] boots to wear.
They are fashionable and stylish, my aunties would be proud
To see my Peppa Pig creation, I stand out in a crowd!

I march around like a sentry guard protecting the Queen!
In these wellie [1] boots, my smile is broadest ever seen.
So a big thank you, for my Mum for getting Dad to buy,
My new wellies [1] so I can walk, run and splash with joy, I cry!

Note: [1] wellies: Is a common word in colloquial UK English for "a pair of wellington boots."

Catherine Caterpillar

My name is Catherine Caterpillar,
I lead a very grubby life!
In leafy lanes,
I crawl along,
Eating as I go.
As I grow old,
I get "kind-a" fat,
Digesting as I move!
Into my hammock,
I snuggle,
As a chrysalis,
I juggle.
Then suddenly my life changes—
My body alters
And, re-arranges!
I wake up as a butterfly,
So, beautiful and sweet, am I!

Baby girl starts to learn

As one is added, one falls down,
You smile, then, join in with a frown,
As if to say, I must try again
To make that building block remain.
You try to stack a bright red one now.
It stays in place; you wave your hands, wow!
Your eyes and mouth open wide with joy,
Learning and playing with your latest toy.

Looking pleased sitting in your special chair,
You gently wave your locks of red hair,
Showing off thin eyebrows over your forehead,
Like stencilled lines that are also coloured red!
You smile and your eyelids flutter,
Pursing your lips as if to mutter:
"It was fun to play building bricks,
Especially now I can stack up six."

You are drawn to the sunlight and shadow,
Moving in the breeze outside your window,
Enticing you to leave your special chair,
And look through the window, over there.
You take in the splendid autumnal scene,
Of orange, red and brown scattered on the green.
Oh, you smile I am so glad I'm me
There's so much to enjoy; so much to see!

Sheep at night

Have you ever seen, a flock of sheep by night
All seated on the ground? If so, it is an amazing sight,
As they stand and feed just like in the daytime,
Even when it's dark and there is no moonshine:
Berr, Berr, Berr that hungry bleating sound.

Oh fluffy creatures grazing quietly in the field
You chew without a sound, with lips politely sealed.
You are never alone, always, with family and friends,
eating
Such concentrated masticating, uninterrupted by
bleating:
Baa Baa Baaaaa, Baa Baa Baaaaa!

When there is a stranger or some other danger near,
Your bleat goes up a pitch, also louder faster, we hear!
Your group encircles the lambs and pregnant ewes:
Huddling together for protection, is the way you
choose:
Merr, Merr, Merrrrh, Merr, Merr, Merrrrh!

If the danger is a fox or larger canine coming to hunt
you,
You bleat even is even more urgent, that is what you do!
You sometimes have been known to stamp your feet,
To call your leading Ram to butt and meet that
predator, to defeat:

Mehrr, Mehrr Mehrrrrh, Mehrr, Mehrr, Mehrrrrh!

But if you are alone till dawn grazing in that field,
With shepherd and your collie dog as your shield,
You go round and round and through the gate,
Not, a sound, you make save of that to masticate:
Mmm, Mmm, Mmmm, Mmm, Mmm, Mmmm!

When something disturbs you from your herbal meal,
You heave a sigh and let out a cry of how you feel.
Then not one but all of you harmonise and croon,
"Leave us be, we want to graze in peace" you bleat in
tune:
Baa Baa Baaaaah, Baa Baa Baaaaaah!

The bleat changes, in volume pitch and key,
With you mood and when you are anxious by what you
see.
In the springtime when the lambs play all night and
day,
Gambolling, skipping, jumping, singing, laughing all
the way: Mayrrh, Mayrrh, Mayrrh, Mayrrh, Mayrrh,
Mayrrh!

When your shepherd arrives, with his collie dog called
Lass,
You know it is time to move to another patch of grass.
You follow over hill and vale, walking, running,
jumping.
The sound you make is now rather like yomping:
Baa, Baa, Baaa, Baa, Baa, Baaa!

Dreams

What is a dream my Granddaddy?
An ideal you'd like to attain, young lady.
What sort of things can we have in a dream?
Why all things are possible my little queen.

Like wanting chocolate truffles and honey?
If you like you can wish for the weather to be sunny,
I wish I could dance on Grandma's favourite TV show,
Then you can try, "Strictly, keep on dancing, you know!"

Do dreams ever come true my Granddaddy?
Sometimes they do my dear young lady.
Only sometimes, why can't all dreams come true?
If they did there would be no dreaming to do!

Which are the ones are most likely to come true?
That is the fun we cannot tell which ones do.
But you can do things to help them along,
By always being happy and doing no wrong.

But how can being happy, help make my dreams come true?
Because that's the magic of dreams, for someone like you!

The ladybird guard

Your spots are handsome and black, on a red bodice,
Somewhat like a soldier, with poise and grace,
No weapons here; they are left locked in the pound!
For you no longer fear, peace in all life, you have
found!

Granddad's best dream

I had a dream when I was a young man.
I dreamt of a kind, beautiful woman like your Gran.
That we would meet, fall in love and marry,
And be happy ever after; your, Grandma and me!
Well Granddad, I know that your dream has come true,
I can see it in the eyes of the both Grandma and you!

The beetle in service

Black as night, camouflaged you stalk about,
Always ready for a fight, unperturbed no doubt,
By others who are creeping and shadow crawling,
Like terrorists or other things appalling!
Proud to be a beetle, fortunate and brave
Prepared to take on all who improperly behave!

The meadow thistle

A wild flowering plant with a fan-tailed apparition,
A mix of green leaves and purple flowers, a sensation!
Forming a display like an amorous peacock's tail,
Without the deafening call of its plaintiff wail!
If you're brushed aside by your lover, his skin will
bristle,
Showing him you really are the pretty meadow thistle!

Meadow time

Have you ever told the time, using nature's clock,
A dandelion head full of parachuted seed stock,
By gently blowing the seeds, to count the hour!
6 puffs later, it's 6 o'clock, by flower power.

I smiled, "daisies are white, buttercups yellow",
Wild orchids are mauve and blue. I'm a lucky fellow,
To wander, meandering, in this meadow of beauty,
And take in the atmosphere, free from toll, tax or
duty.

I could observe from near, and to gaze from afar,
Just to see how wonderful the wild bloomers are!
So quiet and inspiring, I do delight in this place,
This timeless meadow always brings a smile to my
face!

Whiling away the time by watching the seeds float by;
They look like a model of the clouds, high in the sky!

Walking with Grandma

I have just been for a very long walk
With my grandma who does like to talk.
We went over the fields, crossing a bridle way
With Arthur the dog who wants to play.

We trudged on together, Grandma and me,
Through fields of hay, wheat and barley,
When we saw a small herd or deer ahead,
Would Arthur chase them away, we said.

No, he pretended that they were not there
Arthur's so good he can be taken anywhere,
Unless he is teased by a Labrador's barking,
Then he would respond in a flash. Sparking!

Grandma would tell him to wait and to sit,
Arthur would be happy just watching it,
But when the Labrador comes too close, to us,
Arthur snaps back, oh, making such a fuss!

Quickly the dogs forget their quarrel,
And as we walk on, Arthur spots a squirrel,
But he escapes running up a tree,
Arthur comes back panting so heavily.

Grandma says, Arthur you do look so hot,
And Granddad, I do hope you've filled teapot.
I do really like walking in the countryside
Even if I'm in my push chair, really having a ride!

A noise in the bush

What is that noise in the nearby thicket?

Sounds like a clock that is in a hurry!
Should I take notice or worry?
About such constant rattling,
Worse than gossips prattling!

What sort of creature
Has such a nagging feature?
Chirping almost like a bird,
Always the same word,
Absurd!

On hotter days it is of a higher pitch,
Is it really caused by an itch!
On legs that are rubbed together
Moving faster in hotter weather,

Who is there? Just Mr Cricket!

My great Grandma

I'm told, my Great Grandma lives in a bungalow,
A house with no upstairs: because she walks, so slow.
I first met my Great Grandma in the month of May,
At my Grandma's house, when she had come to stay!

She met me with a smile beneath her mop of white
hair,
Sitting in the centre of the room; comfortable on
Granddad's chair!
She has an interesting face with lines around both her
mouth and big brown eyes,
So expressive, soft and clear, yet happy too, such a
nice surprise!

I tried to get her to play, hide and chase around the
house,
But, even with two walking sticks that cat can't catch
this mouse!
She hides her face behind the chair and cries out loud,
"boo!"
I copied her hide and seek, as I thought it was the
thing to do.

She always liked, she said, to relate stories of the past
to me:
About friends and relations old and new, and how life
used to be!

There was a farmer's maid, who milked the cows in
the early morning,
So that the churns could be filled with that creamy
milk, ready for uploading . . .

. . .On to a lorry at the farmyard gate, to start their
long journey,
To the station, then on to the train, for delivery to the
Dairy:
For the city folk to drink, milk is made especially germ
free,
To keep their teeth and bones, like ours, clean and
healthy!

There was the chimney sweep, always black and
covered with soot,
And his little helper boy who climbed inside the
chimney, foot by foot!
A time when all the engines were driven by steam,
whistling loudly, as the past by,
To warn those watching on the bridge, my soot smuts
might hurt your eye!

My Great Grandma told me stories like these, and all
her yesterdays,
Until I fell into a deep sleep, by her side, in a dreamy
daze
With images in my head about how life was before;
With no internet, mobile phone or locked back-door!

The bluebells in bloom

Half term is here the blue bells are in bloom,
Like an indigo carpet early in June.
Stepney is ready to pull the load,
Climb aboard the observation coach.
"Clickety click", the bogeys whisper to the track,
As baby sleeps soundlessly, on the way back!

A working wasp

You sound like a bee, well so nearly,
Except your emotions you show clearly.
Your buzz, when you leave the nest,
Is business-like when you search for zest!
On your return your sound is a tired one,
Carrying, a full load of nectar and pollen!
Buzz, buzz buzz
Buzz, buzz buzz

I, too work in the same garden,
Digging weeds, and carrying with arms fully laden.
I put some onto a compost heap,
From which strong smelling liquids seep!
It was here where tired paths crossed,
You took offence, your tempers lost!
Buzz, buzz BUZZZ!
Buzz, buzz BUZZZ!

Smash into my forehead, you crash diver!
Buzzing away, you shout, "I am a survivor!"
As your buzz comes closer, "ouch, I scream"
I also utter words obscene.
Why did you hurt me 'til it shows?
Because our paths crossed I suppose
Buzz, buzz, ouch!
Buzz, buzz ouch
We must look to the future, and not meet again,
On that collision path in sun or rain

I will use my senses to judge your mood,
As to whether you are fetching or carrying food.
And your nest you could highlight,
So I know where it is by my hindsight
Buzz, buzz, wary,
Buzz, buzz scary!

Oh you
eight-legged, wonder.

Oh you eight-legged wonder with legs all around,
How do you know which way you are bound?

My eight feet detect vibrations and by experience, for
sure,
I can tell what it is and how far away using each foot
sensor!
I can also tell which way it moves, and if a friend or
foe,
So I can determine in which direction to go.

Oh you eight-legged wonder do you run
To catch your prey! How is it done?

You have not been paying attention,
Running I use mainly as a defensive action.
For my food I ensnare a suitable prey!
In a cleverly concealed web, I made earlier today!

Oh you eight-legged wonder do you ever fight,
Or attack other creatures? You look as though you
might.

My looks may frighten, but they can be deceptive,
Me! Looking fierce is what my defence is.
I will only fight when my family is in danger,

Or perhaps for a lover or mate I will wager.

*Oh you eight-legged wonder do you live happy ever
after,
Obviously not I can tell by your laughter?*

Happy or sad are the same to me; I need more prey
To feed my young ones, when, they are born later
today.
And if there is not enough food, my mate will take,
Me as a last resort substitute for the family cake!

*Oh you eight-legged wonder such things you do,
People could learn a lot from you?*

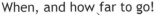

Don't put down your human kind, my growing child,
You can learn from your world, both meek and wild.
Use your senses well and you will instinctively know
What you must do,
When, and how far to go!

Sheep in clover

With white ball shaped flowers and juicy leaves, so
green,
You are a grazing animals' delicate wanton dream!
Cattle will butt each other for a taste
Of that delicious vegetable: without waste.
But the animal that enjoys it the most, is the sheep,
Who will eat clover until they sleep!

They have been known to gorge on clover
And lush green grass, then fill up with gas and then fall
over.
The shepherd must put them back on to their feet
And gas expelled, that is not at all sweet,
From their stomachs, oh so big
Sometimes a sheep acts like a pig!

Kylie the cat

Prowling about with that haughty gait,
Turning your head as you wait,
With nose held high,
You watch your subjects pass by.
Oh queenly pussycat, with regal miaoux!
And that oh, so superior purr!
As I stroke your back, the tension goes now
From my neck and furrowed brow!

Our pet dog

Come, we demand,
Stay, we shout,
Sit, we spout,
When he is at hand.

He listens when we call,
It's true to say,
When he wants to play
Our dog obeys us all.

PART TWO

Just one more time: before it's too late

The journey continues as a collection of experiences
from a young adult to a mature older adult.

Just one more time, sighed the lovers intertwined,
To show you are mine
Just one more time, give me one more chance,
Pleaded the suitor at the dance!
Just one more time, let me score the winner and
tell the story,
Sighed, the old man who'd missed out, on former
glory.
Just one more time, said the man in the wheel chair,
It would be nice to walk over there.

Shepherd's delight.

Oh picture in the sky, who paints your face up there?
Who is with you, there, with that obvious artistic flare?
Could be the work of an old master, and his class:
together they can paint faster!

The bright display of prismatic hues, are there, as I
look on
Meeting the clouds as they begin to sink into the
horizon?
Captivated in a kaleidoscope, trapped by the blue
haze,
Can it be the glancing reflection of a sun's beaming
rays.

It is such a magical image, I simply can't forget
The artistic skill required to do justice to a sunset.
Even with the help of technological innovation,
The sunset must be the work of celestial creation!

No wonder it is known as the shepherds' delight,
To see such a pretty sun set, just before start of night!

The symbol of the rose

There are many kinds of roses that we can grow
Those that ramble small and fat, those that climb, and
also
Tall and slim: They come in many different hues,
From black to white, yellow to red and even blues.

There are many different fragrances; mainly sweet.
Used by men to attract friend or foe so they can meet.
The bloom is worn by men to symbolise sorrow at
death and strife,
And to represent, at happier times, a partnership for
life!

The rose is such a visibly powerful, symbolic tool.
But here's a warning, that rose is no man's fool!
It is man that flirts with danger: from war to pollution,
Global warming, new disease: even retribution?

He, alone must choose his fate and how he lives,
Hate or love, war or peace, all or nothing, takes or
gives.
The Rose cares not for what he chooses, it will last for
ever
But man has power to exist or self-destruct, but
never—

Will be returned to that Rose Garden in Eden land,

With ambrosia, nectar and sweet scents forever at hand!
For only the blood red roses remain, under the midday sun.
And man is no longer living there, to see what he has done!

Spider's web

While walking through wild orchid meadow,
One very warm day in July
I came across a spider's web, on show,
So big it took me, two seconds to walk by!

It must have spanned eight foot by ten:
A cover sheet over rye grass, and flowers!
I stopped and stared and stared again!
Its intricacies kept my mind entranced for hours.

I closed my eyes in reverie, head spinning like a top.
I marvelled at the web and its immense spread,
With lattice work small enough to trap, a water drop.
Overall it was larger than a king sized double bed!

I dreamt of dryads, pixies, nymphs and the fairy
queen,
Of the white rabbit, mad hatter, dormouse and Alice.
Of Sirens luring sailors to the rocks, with sights, to
some, obscene!
Then I opened my eyes to see a spider angry and full of
malice!

The builder of the web appeared, he was about two
feet long,
With eyes, as big as saucers, and the jaw as big as an
Alsatian dog!
Pouncing, he held me down with his eight legs strong,

As I struggled to get free, I slipped over a fallen log.

As I stumbled back to my feet, I opened my eyes wide,
I rubbed them once and twice, and then once more.
The spider now was smaller, only two inches along its side.
His legs were not so strong now, but my ankle was very sore!

My heart is heavy with remorse to see what I had achieved,
If I had left the web alone: we both would have a future.
But, I acted carelessly destroying it: there was no real need!
How much more damage does mankind to Mother Nature?

A queenly visitation

She was there,
I felt a scare,
She was in my face, standing on my bedroom curtain,
I closed and re-opened my eyes, just to be certain,
Of what I saw,
I stood in awe
Of her dangerous beauty, sprinkled with wax from a
mould,
Wrapped up in a sweater with hoops of black and
bright gold!
I felt uneasy
And a little queasy,
At the unannounced visit through my bedroom window,
By the Empress and Queen now here on display, what a
show!
As I got near,
Full of fear,
At her humming sound like a dreaming cat,
I had to run for cover under a mat!
I made a rush,
Ready to crush
Her as I grabbed the curtain underside,
And pushed the window open wide!
Have I the right
To destroy, or put her to flight
To chase her from this resting place, or would I regret
Disturbing the Empress of Wasps, the Queen Hornet?
But I had not the will,

When it came to the kill,
Or to cause her majesty's untimely end!
Instead I shook the curtain: we parted as friends!

The field orchid

Eye catching, sophisticated bloom, growing wild in the meadow
Hidden by grass, so, for you we need to look below,
Among the rye for a ten inch stalk, on display,
For all to see, both night and day!

With your one hundred heads tightly bound
On the tip of your stalk eight inches above the ground.
A choice of petal colours to delight;
Pinkish Mauve and white!

The shape of your blooms, are exquisite.
You're the complete fashion model—you're it!

A knock at my window

While I was relaxing in my favourite chair,
When there was a loud knock at a window over there!
With a shock and a start, I looked out of the window
to see
A bird on the ground; just a pane of glass, away
from me!

It must have really hurt its head,
I would not be surprised if the bird is dead,
If not, it must be in pain. But I feel no sympathy
As the noise had woken me from my reverie!

The blue meadow Butterfly

A pretty pastille blue,
Skipping gently over the grass,
Sampling nature's food and drink,
Do you ever pause to think?

What role you play,
Acting out Nature's scene?
As you feed on flower or even a weed.
Do you ever marvel at the making of a seed?

And how it grows in a flowers hood,
From which you take your food,
And lay your eggs, from which are born
Your offspring so that life continues on!

Until Man destroys you and natures lot,
All for a concrete parking spot!

My favourite aunt

My favourite Aunt is one of life's ladies,
A nurse, who sometimes looks after babies,
Has a very special gift for speaking at dinner,
For engaging everyone's attention she's a real winner!
One day she made a very loud fart just after grace,
It's the sort of thing she can do with a smile on her
face.
She introduces quietly into the conversation,
Talk of bowel habits and similar information.
"You know yesterday it would not come through,"
As she went to the loo for a number two!
Another heave and another strain,
Made me quickly go again!
The other day she had to go,
Not a real dump you know!
It's not the usual kind of story to relate,
With a slice of beef and gravy on your plate!
Well the information about her digestion,
May be an interesting diversion!
But she also likes to talk of her pantie hose and lace,
And, just as you try to hide your embarrassed, face,
Then she continues to talk without any fear!
Too late you've turned bright scarlet from ear to ear!
Oh, my favourite aunt is so charming,
Even though her talk can be alarming!
She means little harm or offence by it:
Better than talking tittle-tattle or bullshit!

My father's ring

Why are you leaving home, why are you going away?
Do think so little of us you want to leave today?
Have we not sacrificed our lives to give you the best!
Is this your way of saying thanks and forget the rest?

I want to see what I can do and achieve,
Now can't you see that's the reason why I must leave!
I'm grateful for all you've done, but I'm still under
your spell,
How I listened; but you turned away when I had words
to tell!

But you are so young, there's so much to do and learn,
Then let me make my own mistakes and be myself; it's
my turn!
Why make the same mistakes? Oh, you never have
listened to me!
I need to break away from your influence; can't you
see?

No my son, I do not understand why you need to go
away to learn,
But you must! It was you who taught me to go for
what I yearn.
Yearn, learn it doesn't seem that way from my point of
view,
There you go again, you've not listen to a word I said
to you!

I have always known what is best! You were always my concern.
I know that to be so, but it's my independence, I yearn!
Your love is too strong I must be freed from your control,
It is time to go now and I must follow the feelings in my soul!

You said once before you had to break from your father's hold.
Now it is my turn to find out what is out there and be bold.
That is not the same times were much harder then,
And children had to grow quickly into soldier men!

Times are not easier they are just different today,
Yes I can see that is so, but do you have go away?
You can have control of your life, I promise not to interfere
You can be your own man with us, so why not stay here!

I'm sorry father I cannot waste my life away arguing with you,
I must go and take note of that inner voice telling me what to do!
It is with regret I must let you go, but promise me one thing,
You'll always remember us and wear this, my father's ring!

The attraction of cherry blossom.

Oh, wonderful deep pink cherry flower,
How I can sit and admire you hour by hour.
How I wish to taste your nectar sweet,
As your petals part, ready to greet
Me, as if we are long lost friends.
Hungrily I gorge and drink till it ends.
My sacks are filled up to the brim,
And, I am satiated from within.

It's a bumble bees' collection

Your attraction is your scent, so musky and so sweet,
It catches my attention as I fly around to meet
The source of the supply of your heavenly drink,
Needed to fill our honeycombed store to the brink!

I get enjoyment searching hedgerow and the bush,
Looking for the signs of maturity; I'm not in a rush.
Experience will find those flowers, on which I can
settle,
It must be a sturdy one, to support me as I land on its
petal!

Then to alight, I have to be as gentle as I can,
My feet are far more sensitive than any fingertips of
man!
My favourite petal is coloured red, I look for the sign
That the petals are ready to part, revealing that
nectar, so fine!

I sit on the petals edge, waiting for that special
moment;
The release by the flower of a sweeter, addictive
scent,
And the parting petals revealing still more beauty
within,
The anthers and stamens are now ready for me to
enter in!

As I burrow deeper into the flower, the nectar and the pollen
Fill my sacs until they are overflowing, and swollen.
I rest for a while satisfied, then noting the locality as I fly away,
I know where to find that wonderful elixir on another day!

In Love

It has been said men
Think and dream,
Even fantasize,
And eulogize
About a fleeting chance
To have that perfect union
Just once, then again!

I used to flatter myself
I'd never be left on the shelf
I was the one using the library
Choosing from different categories:
Be they Naiads of fact
Dryads of fiction
Or Titania, the fairy queen!

Somehow,
After that our first meet I knew,
I must play it cool.
Before I open another door,
I'd been infatuated before.
But that was when I was young
A time before my Eden had begun.

We became so happy in our world,

Growing close,

Loving each day

Walking in the woods

The meadows

The heather

Together!

The Caravan

In a remote part of Britain, way out on a limb,
Lived three bachelor lads; Dave, Taff and Jim.
In hotels they lived as they worked away from base,
The lads felt bored, they missed the challenge of the
chase!

It was a warm Sunday at the beginning of May,
While out for a drive together on this lovely day,
They saw a sign: new and used caravans are to be sold,
A glance at each other; they were of one mind, let's
buy one: be bold!

So the three bachelor lads, haggled over the price,
Well at least Taff did, as he had fatherly advice.
Terms and conditions were set and price agreed.
They hooked up the caravan, and left with full speed.

They drove to the coast and found a likely spot
In a nearby field! The farmer was keen to rent a plot.
So after the legal formalities, a parking place they
chose
It was next to the beach, with water supplied through
a hose.

The three settled down and got on well together
In that mobile home among the grass, and heather!
The view was a magnificent one, from Golspie to Tain,

Across the Dornoch Firth, always clear except when it
rained!

With working different shifts they only occasionally
met:
So the detail of housekeeping was in itself treated as a
project.
One evening, over a beer or two, Taff and Jim devised
a plan,
And Dave promised to provide whenever when he can.

When together on their day off, it was one of Taff's
suggestions,
To visit a nearby highland town, on Saturdays, for
fishing expeditions!
They often returned with fresh fish or venison, and
once or twice,
They found friendly female company: against Taff's
fathers advice!

This bachelor's paradise had to come to an end,
As Jim and Dave were sent offshore with a friend!
There was another reason; the winter drew near,
It was cold inside and the pub had the fire and beer.

Late winter there was a storm, which blew the caravan
over.
From their employer they borrowed a hoist and
Land-rover,
To pull it back on its wheels it could still be towed!
Pleased they posted a notice: one caravan to be sold!

Then, one a dark night the caravan was taken away,
By a man from the Glasgow Mafia so legends say!
Taff caught up with the Mafiosi tried to broker a deal.
But backed down in time to keep his teeth straight and real!

He stopped the man showing him his Glasgow kiss[2],
And look away in time for the Glasgow smile[3] to miss.
But he said "No, I did you a favour taking it away for free:
The bodywork was dented and when it rained, it was leaky!"

So that was the end of the mobile bachelor pad,
Whose demise and parting was anything but sad.
But they still remember smiling, the days that were fun;
Like the time they were chased by the man with the shotgun!

Notes:
(2) Glasgow kiss: Urban Glaswegian for a head butt.
(3) Glasgow smile: Urban Glaswegian for a facial scar from being cut on the edge of the mouth, resembling an extended smile.

The Hen Party

My girl-friend went up to London,
With a party dress and make up on,
To a concert in Hyde Park, oh boy!
To sing and dance, and to enjoy,
With a bunch of girls, a hen party,
All dressed up, happy and hearty!

While the party carried on,
She to the loo had gone!
When she finished her ablutions,
She got lost, what is the solution?
When her mobile phone she tried,
Only to find the battery had died!

Cannot see my contact names and addresses,
Thinks my friend," what a mess this is!"
Thousands of people in Hyde Park,
She searched for her friends until dark.
The time was getting later and later, all alone
My girl-friend began to make her way home.

When she got to the underground,
She didn't have a clue: what's Camden Town?
It was to Victoria she had to go,
But because her watch was slow,
When she arrived the board did say,
The last train home had already left today!

To the taxi rank she went,
All her money now she spent.
But she got home 80 minutes later,
To see her flat mates waiting for her.
My girl—friend says, "lessons have I learned":
Make sure your phone is fully charged.

And when you are in a strange place, and need to find the loo,
There is safety in numbers, go with a friend, making two!
And when there are a lot of people all around,
For advice ask a policeman, in such a strange surround!
And when you go to a strange venue
Always have prepared a getting home menu!

A quiet misty morning

Four a. m. and all is quiet,
Not, a soul, to cause a riot.
Only as I peer through a white gazebo,
I can hear the sound of pigeons calling, "hello,
It's time to get up and sing deeply,
Let's make a noise and wake up the sleepy."
We are searching for food and chattering
Through that mist shroud so damp and clinging.

Have you heard the sound of pigeons calling,
"Coo coo-eee"? loudly in your ears; early in the
morning!
All I want is the farmers shot gun,
To shoot them all! Not one by one!
For waking me from my dreamy slumber,
Will I ever know what happens, I wonder,
In my dream from which I was disturbed
Through the mist, by that noisy varmint of a bird!

Five a.m. all is still,
Look there's a kestrel going for the kill.
It's over there, where? Damn this misty morning,
For hiding one of nature's sights, beneath an awning,
By surrounding all with that dampening overcoat:
Showing ghostly scenes that seem; somehow, remote.
But still the white blanket, cannot hide the sound,
Of those damned pigeons calling over the ground.

My pet dog is a welsh border collie,
Watches the lambs play in folly.
He sits alone and without expression and is aloof,
Halfway up the stairway to the garage roof.
He looks puzzled; he cannot see them clearly,
Through nature's lace curtain, "yes I can, well nearly!
Look at me I'm the king of the castle,
Not some noisy coo, cooing rascal!"

Six a.m. and all has gone,
The mist has lifted the day has begun,
What was that with wings that flap so loudly,
It's that varmint pigeon coo cooing proudly.
I snap, I've had enough of being woken up so early,
I call the farmer with his shot gun who nearly
Shoots the pigeon, but just misses this time,
I want to finish my dream, is that such a crime?

The harbingers
of the future

Can the future be foretold by gazing at the stars?
Does Venus really have influence over Mars?
Can our emotions be affected by bodies floating in
space?
Can the rising moon stir passion in this very place?
Do you wake when the full moon brings such influence
and light?
Does the moonshine heighten your perception during
that night?

Some have the gift to communicate into another
world,
Guided by a little knowledge of your past—your story
they unfurled!
Some can read your fortune in the dregs of a tea cup,
Some can read the future using Tarot cards, or is it all
made up?
Some can see a new journey in the heart of a crystal
ball,
By gazing at tomorrow's light reflected back, revealing
all.

The harbingers of the future can only foretell what is
true,
If you let them influence your tomorrow in what you do!

The early morning birds

On an early-morning 4 a.m. in June,
The sound of birds filled my room with tune.
I steered and listened in awe and wonder
At the sounds that awoke me from my slumber.

It was like a chattering of whistles
Among the hedgerows, meadows grass and thistles
As I know began listen intently,
To hear what the whistling meant to me.

A lonely whistle rang out in alarm!
"Where's my lover?" "I've returned, no harm."
Just then a pigeon coo-cooed with concern,
"Where is our son? Out all night: he'll learn."

And then as if is to reply a gang friends appear
"Great night out boys, 'bye, okay mum I'm here.
A cheeky pigeon slowed as she passed by, and cooed
"Thank you for the good time you handsome dude!

A loud low pitched call then I heard
It was a crow calling for a meeting how absurd.
A laughing Jay was overheard remarking:
It's another forum with no purpose: just squawking!

But the crow continued with its meeting call
Until there was a quorum on my garden wall!
A warning from a Jackdaw lookout brought about a
premature ending,

As a deafening flock of starlings swept by:
the noise was overwhelming!

I put my head under the pillow like going to ground
To protect my ears from this horrible squawking sound!
From out of the sky came the loud chorus sound
Of thousands of starlings swarming and swooping
down!

Eventually I fell asleep, but was re-awaken by these
words
"Your late, get up for work it's after eight," your alarm
birds!

A Seasonal view

I look from my garden using my eyes and ears, as video lens,
This scene is a window on to my life, loves and friends!

In the springtime nature's new generations appear,
Both animal and plant life are content and show no fear!
White and yellow flowers are scattered on the grassy floor.
Each living thing begins to stir and ask why, and do more!
Insects hum, birds sing and baby lambs gambol about,
Parents smile and watch their children run and shout!
The trees surround the scene with their colourful bloom,
Of pink and white, long forgotten is the feeling of wintry gloom.

It's summer now, the trees blooms, such a rich green hue,
Just like a picture frame they surround and retain the view.
The baby lambs, quieter now have grown into young sheep.
The birds wake us early with their chatter from our sleep!
The sunlight and the shadows all mixed in an artist's pot,

With gleams that twinkle all the day, making it seem hot!
The birds have flown the nest to flock with their friends,
And insects are busy collecting, buzzing until the day ends!

In autumn, the leaves are red, orange and ruddy-brown.
And the wind sometimes howls, making the leaves fall down,
On to the green, beneath the trees to complete the tapestry, dampened by the morning mists, that ebb and flow in front of me.
Some sheep have been to market where they were sold,
While those that remain, huddle to keep warm from the cold.
All animals have to prepare to face the winter close at hand,
While, some birds prepare for a journey to warmer lands!

Winter arrives with Jack Frost carrying his white paint brush
To mark every blade of grass, branch and twig in a rush!
Hares and rabbits are safe, shut in their homely burrow,
To spend the next 2 months, sleeping for tomorrow!

Then the snow covers all, completing Jack Frost's scene:
A solitary fox leaves his footprints to show where he's been!
All else is still, except for the activity of man,
Dominating the scene as nature takes a rest while she can!

The sunlight warms the last wintry days, melting the snow,
The cycle comes round again, wherever did yesterday go?
The scrawny fox can look forward to regular feeding,
Thanks to the plants in the food chain re-seeding.
I can meet some old friends: the robin, squirrel, fox and hare,
And the pet dogs with their walkers are there.
Snap the shutter closes, on the colours and sounds of last year,
Just in time for a repeat of what was before and soon to re-appear!

I have no special thing

It's a shame to tell, I have no special thing,
No memento about which I could sing,
Or even tell a story to tell and shout,
Because it's company I care about.

It's true to say many hobbies I've had,
From collecting coins and train-spotting, how sad!
When grown up I thought I always knew the score.
I've played many sports and watched even more,

I've enjoyed many of life's sights and sounds of live
matches and concerts, at many grounds,
And been excited by many kinds of racing;
Even had a flutter on steeple-chasing!

I've enjoyed many simple pleasures in good company,
To talk and debate for fun mainly, you see.
So this is my special thing to have people to listen to;
Hah there goes the door-bell; I do hope it's you!

A silvery trail

It was a warm, sultry evening in June,
I saw a silvery trail, lit up by the moon.
I was intrigued; I could not wait until tomorrow.
I removed by shoes and socks and began to follow,
That silvery trail, forward, around and around!
I was treading carefully trying not to make a sound!

"But, yuck!" I cried, "In what, have I just trodden?
A cold clammy mess, my feet were sodden.
My reaction was to take another stride,
And place it down again, I could have died!
Not again, I put my foot into another squidgy place,
I was alone, except for the moon shining in my face!

I stopped and looked down on the ground,
And I open mouthed, the source I found.
I watched a black juicy slug, it was obscene!
It was eating a newly planted, green runner bean!
In fact I stopped and looked again, I swore!
Not one but a herd fat black slugs I saw.
I ran away in shock and horror at my plight,
Washed my feet, now I was ready for the fight.

So I made a plan to keep them from my seeds,
Around the vegetable patch I put some weeds,
And in between some poison especially prepared,
Not one of those slugs would I let be spared!

Next day, I was surprised to see that the poison had all gone,
But did I see any of those slugs? No not even one,
They had eaten all my newly planted vegetable seeds
But incidentally they ate all but the newly planted weeds!

November view

As I gaze out on to the moonlight November view,
Across meadow and woodland evoke in me, thoughts of you,
Reflected in the soft orange light in the shade,
Our emotions quiet like the stillness of the everglade.

I think of how our retirement years should have been
Like a colourful autumnal leafy lane, the artists favoured scene.
Instead I see the still, deserted, autumnal night,
Of scattered bushes and wooded copses, an unwelcoming sight.

Oh, how I wish we could wake together on a beautiful autumn morn,
Cosy, warm and happy, in the thought, that a new day is born.
From beneath the rolling mist, the frost melts from the meadow,
Glistening in the sunlight: a kaleidoscope of colours and broken shadows!

My eyes search for you in the moonlit and sunlit landscape scene:
Within the quiet stillness, hoping to tempt you back from where you've been,
Into this the cheerful room both within and without of me.

I'm still yearning for that glimpse of thee.

But you are not seen, still lost in the shadow,
Even as gaze into the moonlit night, from my window.

From my window

I feel so quiet.
It is so still.
I am calm.
I feel tranquil.
Smiling, I gaze from my window.
All is asleep.
Is my gaze invasive?
All is in place,
Is my gaze offensive?
Unperturbed, I gaze from my window.
Shapes appear,
My thoughts confide.
Shapes sway about,
My thoughts are taken for a ride.
Mesmerised, I dream as I look from my window.
Bird song fills the air.
I listen to the tunes they make.
Dogs bark out loud.
I hear the dawn break.
Astonished, I wake before my window.
Engines burst into life,
My head fills with sound
Man causes commotion,
My head spins around.
I stretch, in front of my window.

Crossing an ocean

If you find it hard to relax try floating on the world's
oceans,
This can be very soothing, if you have troubled
emotions!
Don't take a trip on a busy trawler or town sized ocean
liner,
But on board a Super-tanker there is no peacefulness
that is finer.

You can float for days or even weeks of tranquillity on
the calm sea
You can solve many issues in your mind, without
conflict or hostility.
What if there is a gale, hurricane or storm, look does
the barometer fall?
What can you do but wait and see what nature has in
mind, that's all.

You have time to prepare yourself in an appropriate
way,
For predicting the path of storms is relatively easy to
do today!
But you as a passenger have already ceded control of
your fate,
So relax as you cross the oceans, the future will have
to wait!

Out of Love

I do not know what spoiled our Eden
We were happy together,
Could be forever?
Then the roses grew no more.
Love faded quietly
Setting slowly
Like the winter sun.

My eyes wandered,
Over the garden fence,
And to the village allotment
I caught a glimpse
I re-focused,
Un-discussed,
Still I did as must!

Oh Shame!
I wish I could recall
When I lost my heart
To a nymph
With assets to steal anyone's love away:
Attractive
Both Interactive and Proactive!

I tried to rediscover the plough
And the magic seeds,
Alas all I see are weeds!
I live in hope

Need optimism to cope,
Best to wait and see,

I tried once again
To return to my Eden,
Just one more time!

PART THREE

Just one more time . . . It's too LATE?

An aging adult who is near the end of his allotted time getting ready or not as he chooses, for the start of a new journey, if it exists.

Just one more time, let me say what I should have before,
Prayed the man still waiting at death's door!
Just one more time, make my muscles and mind obey my brain,
Prayed Parkinson's man, so I can be understood again!
Just one more time let me communicate with the one I love.
Prayed the man with Dementia to his God above!
Just one more time I need help too
Prayed the man who was ready but was waiting for you

Caring Moments.

Can you recall the first time I would ask
for help to do a specific task
like putting on a shirt, or straightening a tie.
Buttons were difficult, do you remember why?

The first time you dried me after a bath,
Caused so much enjoyment , oh what a laugh!
Then my chin was cut when you first helped me to
shave,
you smiled, and said you were becoming my slave.

Yes there were times when caring was fun.
It was doing the other things when the difficulties
come!
It was then we discovered the hard side of caring
living too close, and forced into all sharing!

Recall: you knocked that china statue from the shelf,
Was also the day when you first wet yourself!
Other days when you could no longer dress
or when you soiled your pants, oh what a mess!

How can I forget my first loss of dignity;
People smiling looking on; such a shame and a pity!
But I also recalled the love that we shared
Is still within our hearts, as we publically dared

......to smile at our adversity,
and show our love demonstrably,
by caressing and cuddling each other so closely
but being together was enough for us, mostly!

Thank you to a special carer

Thank you to a special Carer,
Thank you for being my nurse,
My housemaid, and my cook,
My batman and my chauffeur,
And my eyes when I forget to look!

Thank you to a special Carer,
Thank you for being my gardener,
My gamekeeper, and laundry maid,
My char lady and housekeeper,
And my memory for things I've mislaid!

Thank you to a special carer
Thank you for being my e-mailer,
My telephonist and my doorman,
My Lasting Power of Attorney
And my good ears I can call on!

Thank you to a special carer
Thank you always being there
For helping me when I need care,
As my partner or my cell mate
Or just friend with whom I can relate!

My Senses and You

I'm glad I've got a sense of touch,
To feel your love, oh, so much!
I'm glad I've got a sense of smell,
To sense you close makes me swell.
I'm glad I've got a sense of taste,
With my tongue I savour you, without haste
I'm glad I've got a sense of sight,
To see you makes me think, you might?
I'm glad I've got a sense of hearing,
'cause I can hear when you're coming!
With my senses I can love you,
More than words can do.

If I ever lose my sense of touch,
Then I won't feel, but you can do such.
If I ever lose my sense of smell,
Then you will have my scent to tell.
If I ever lose my sense of taste,
You will have to taste in my place!
If I ever lose my sense of sight,
I cannot see you but think of you still might!
If I ever lose my sense of hearing
You will be quiet but still appealing
Without senses, I have no feeling
But with your love I'm happy being

The loss of a faithful friend

John, I was saddened to hear of your loss of your
friend,
On whom you had come so much to depend:
As a companion, a guardian and like-minded soul,
Who enjoyed, very much, taking you for a stroll.
Do you remember that precocious young thing,
Would never perform in the training ring,
So you'd trained him in the woods to stand,
Walk, sit, come and heel, at your command.

And when you rewarded him his favourite treat,
He would laugh his pants off, in doggie speak!
The first time he ventured out on his first shoot,
He returned with a pheasant right to your boot!
Of the time when you were best gun of the day,
His chest swelled with pride, for you, might say.
You recall that he loved to work hard on the beat,
Before snuggling by the fire and lying on your feet.

About the times you played together, such fun,
On those countryside evenings, in the sun,
And beating the bounds now is a lifetime away,
But you can recall all you did with him before today.
So when you are a little sad, perhaps, now and again,
Think of me your gundog, workmate and friend,

Remember the 15 years of happiness, you had together:
Just you, walking with him through the blossoming heather!

The Lady who . . .

The young lady who made a beautiful bride
Welcomed, all, with arms opened wide.
The young lady who was a devoted wife,
Stayed with her partner the rest of his life!
The young lady who liked to sing and dance,
Was our Mum, so full of love and romance!

The married lady who raised a family of six,
Made the simply the best Irish stew mix.
The married lady who cared for us when we fell ill,
Made clothes for us knitting with such skill.
The married lady who loved us when we did wrong
Always gave us somewhere to belong.

The lady who gave us the key to the door,
Encouraged us to always do more!
The lady who was cheerful when things were good,
At times was occasionally misunderstood.
The lady who when Dad was ill and died,
Needed cheering up when she cried.

The old lady who quickly made up her mind,
Was cantankerous but always kind,
The old lady who was sometimes depressed,
Was liked, because she tried her best!
The old lady who recently passed away,
Was our Mum, whose life we celebrate today!

The last train on 11th November 2010

The last train to Sheffield Park descends, Freshfield
Bank, with ease,
In the evening sun passing by one of the lonely mature
oak trees.
The train and tree together are silhouetted, eclipsed
on the horizon,
Wrapped by a cummerbund of cloud, that scatters
gleams from the sun.

There are pink and violet tints within the vast evening
sky of blackened blues,
And some scattered yellow, orange and red striations
of spectral hues.
The sunset colours are reminiscent of those inside a
furnace for making steel,
With white and orange colours in the smoke reflecting
the warm feel.

The engine, coaches and track are made from joined
steel components,
That had been hammered into shape by a skilled
artisan, in a quite a few moments.
The puffs of smoke from Engine number one, four,
seven, three
Demonstrate what little effort is needed, as she
passed by the tree.

The autumnal oak with leaves of blood red and brown,
eclipsed on the sunset:
The image, captured on November the eleventh,
lingers on, lest we all forget!

Passing on

Alone I sit under the setting sun,
Recalling what I have done.
Of living sometimes with fun,
And what I have become
Does it really matter?
It's only whispers and chatter?

I feel that I'm changing,
By mind is re-arranging,
No longer am I raging,
In preparation of staging,
Putting everything in sequence,
I recall my life experience.

I feel detachment, as it flashes past,
I will very soon to breathe my last
I have had my time my dies have been cast,
I feel my spirit fading fast!
Just one more time, just once again? I cry
But my spirit is going, going, gone . . . .